Nature CLOSE-UPS

Cicada Sing-Song

- Text and photographs by Densey Clyne -

Gareth Stevens Publishing
MILWAUKEE

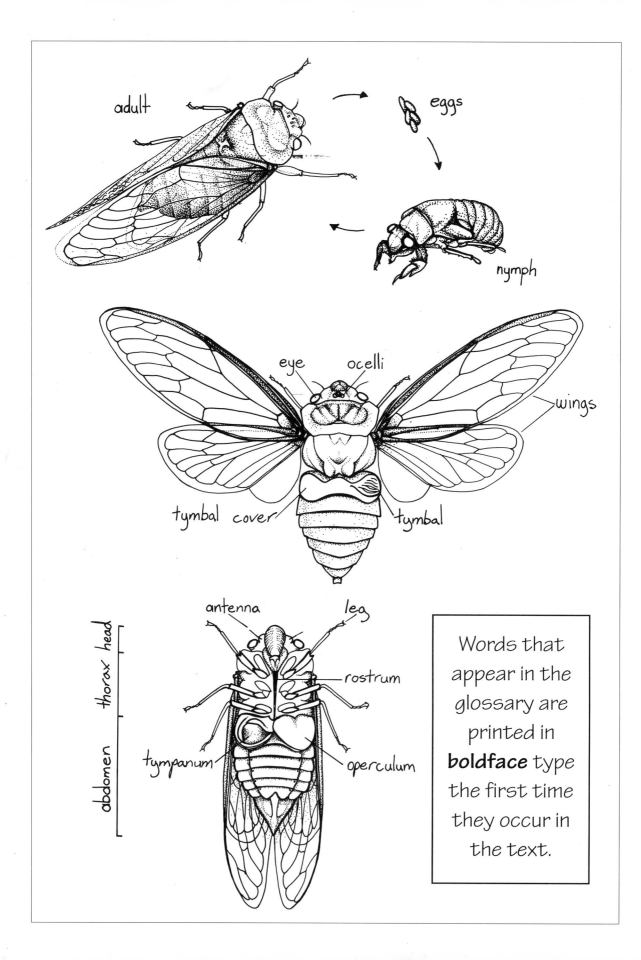

adult

eggs

nymph

eye   ocelli

wings

tymbal cover   tymbal

antenna   leg

head

thorax

rostrum

abdomen

tympanum   operculum

Words that appear in the glossary are printed in **boldface** type the first time they occur in the text.

The sound of summer

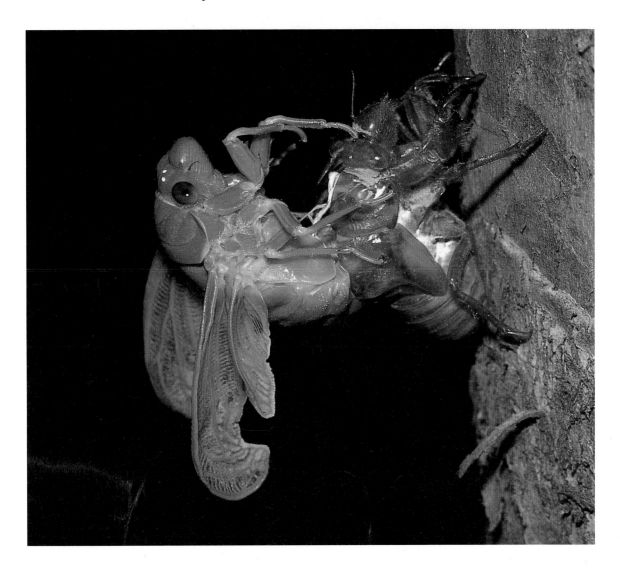

On a warm summer night, a cicada casts off its skin, or shell, and gets ready for the final stage of its life. After years of living underground, it will soon be flying and feeding in the sunshine with other cicadas of its kind. If it is a male, it will sing an incredibly loud song.

The sound made by cicadas in summer is the loudest sound made by any insect. When cicadas sing together in a chorus, the volume is powerful.

When cicadas sing, the sound is loud even to them. They must adjust their **eardrums** to avoid deafening themselves.

In tropical climates, cicadas sing all year long. But in areas of the world where winters are cool, they sing only in summer.

The steady shrilling of greengrocer cicadas, or green Mondays, is one of the common sounds of summer. Usually, cicadas sing in the daytime, but during a heat wave, they may keep it up far into the night.

Some of the greengrocer types are actually yellow-orange in color. They are called yellow Mondays (*above, right*). They are not as common as green Mondays, which are green in color (*above, left*).

Cicadas share the treetops with their worst enemies — birds — so they need to be able to hide from them. Cicada coloring blends well with the greens and browns of leaves and tree trunks. So when cicadas stay still, they are well **camouflaged**. A cicada's loud call also keeps birds away.

Feeding time

Cicadas feed on a
juice, called sap, found in
trees. The red-eye
cicada (*above*) is
feeding on the sap of a
gum tree. It draws in
the sap through a
drinking tube in its body.

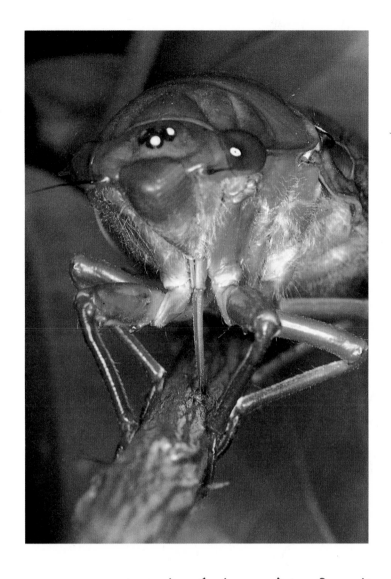

The greengrocer cicada (*above*) is feeding. You can see its drinking tube stuck into the branch. The tube is called a **rostrum**, or beak. It has a sharp point at the end to penetrate the bark, and a hinge at the top so that it can fold back against the cicada's body when not in use.

The sharp point of the rostrum is harmless to people and other animals.

The cherry nose cicada (*below*) looks as though it has a big red nose, but it is not a nose. It is actually a group of muscles. These muscles pump sap up through the rostrum and into the cicada's body.

Insects, such as the cicada, do not need noses. They detect scents through sense organs on their **antennae** and legs. Sense organs also are located around their mouths. Insects have a very good sense of smell.

Sights and sounds

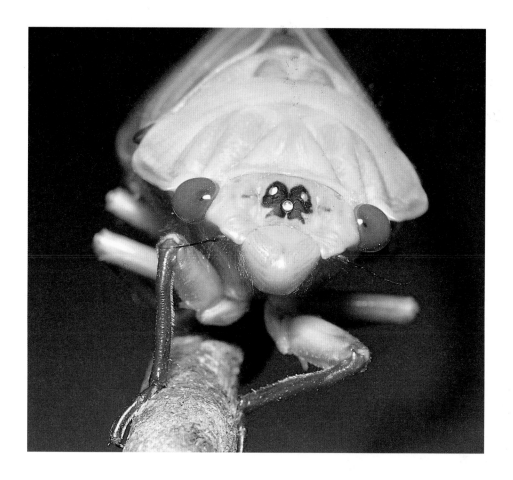

One of the most noticeable features of the cicada is its two large, shining eyes. It also has three little eyes between the two big ones. These small ones are called ocelli, which simply means "little eyes." Ocelli detect only light and darkness, but they probably also help an insect determine the shapes of trees and other large objects in its flight path.

A cicada's ears are quite different from a human's. They are not on its head, and they do not stick out. But like a human, the cicada has two eardrums, called **tympani**. On a cicada, these are hidden under the big flaps visible when a cicada is on its back (*above*). These protective flaps are called **operculi**. The operculi are bigger in the male cicada than in the female.

Timpani is also the name for large, round, kettledrum types of percussion instruments. But drums do not hear sounds; they produce sounds. The male cicada produces sounds with its **tymbals**.

The cicada's tymbals lie on both sides of the tympani. They are hidden away under rigid flaps called tymbal covers.

A male cicada has two pairs of flaps — operculi that cover the tympani, and the smaller tymbal covers that cover the tymbals.

The male cicada's abdomen is almost completely hollow. It acts as a **resonating** chamber to make its song louder. The female, however, needs this space in her abdomen for egg-production.

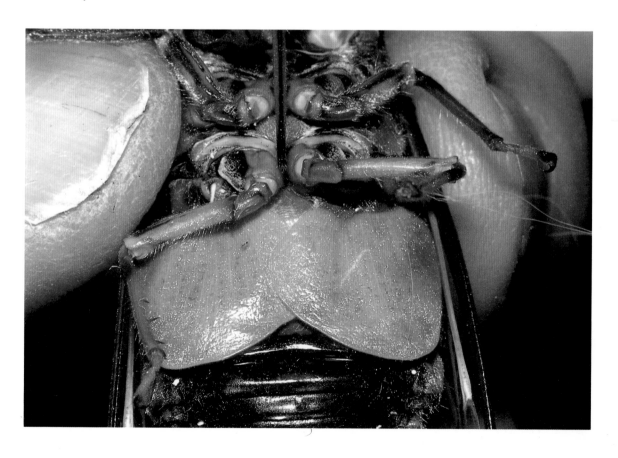

From egg to adult

Cicadas do not always have wings and live in trees. They spend most of their lives under the ground. But how does a young cicada first get underground?

This adult female (*left*) is laying her eggs. You can see her ovipositor, or egg-placer, stuck in the bark of a stem. It looks like a black needle, and it has a sharp, sawlike tip. As the female moves up or down the stem, the ovipositor cuts a series of slits and injects eggs into them. These slits form safe **incubators** for the eggs until they hatch.

Greengrocers and a few other cicadas lay their eggs in dead sticks. The rest lay them into living green wood. When branches from gum trees fall, you can sometimes find stems with slits in them (*right*), but they are usually empty.

Some cicadas place several eggs into each slit (*right*). Others lay only two or three eggs.

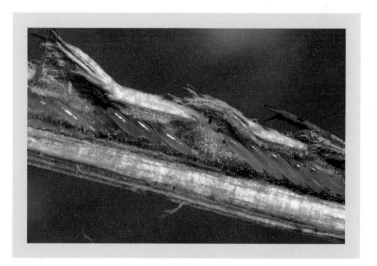

After a while, tiny cicada **nymphs** hatch from the eggs. They cannot fly, and it would take them a long time to walk down the tree trunk, so they simply drop out of the tree. The nymphs are so tiny they almost float down and land without hurting themselves. At this stage in their lives, there is more danger of being eaten by **predators** than of injury from the fall.

When a nymph reaches the ground, it **burrows** into the soil. Underground, it sticks its rostrum into a small root of the tree it fell from and feeds. Nymphs **molt** four times.

When a nymph grows too big for its burrow, or needs a larger root to feed on, it tunnels down farther. The nymph's waste fluids strengthen the soft walls of the burrow.

As time goes by, perhaps one year or perhaps many, the cicada nymph grows bigger and bigger. Then one day, it starts moving upward through the soil. Just below the surface, it stops. It waits there for the right kind of weather for the journey above ground.

When conditions are right, out it creeps. It is dirty and often muddy from the damp burrow.

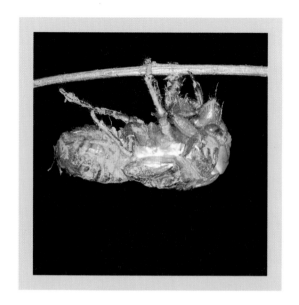 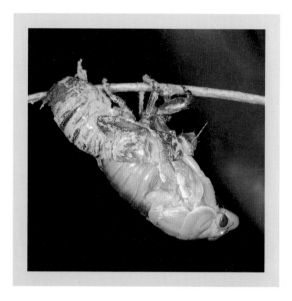

The cicada climbs the nearest tree, shrub, or even garden fence. It stops just a short distance from the ground. Its front claws, specialized for burrowing, have a new job now (above).

They hold the cicada safely in place until its transformation is complete.

Inside a slit behind the cicada's head, the smooth, new skin of the adult is visible. The cicada puffs itself up to force its head and thorax through the widening slit (above).

The new legs must be pulled out slowly and carefully because they could easily break.

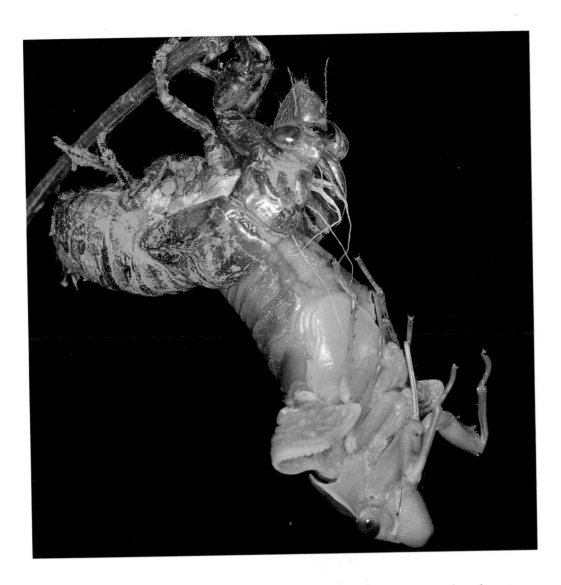

Once its head, thorax, legs, and crumpled wings are free, the cicada bends far back, attached to its old skin only by the tip of its body (*above*).

Notice the stringlike objects hanging out of the old shell. These are the linings of the mouthparts, breathing tubes, and anus.

All of these body parts will be replaced during molting.

Winging it

With the cicada hanging upside-down (*top*), the rostrum is visible between the bases of its six legs. That is where it is kept between meals, out of the way.

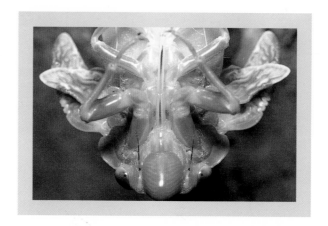

After years of being scrunched up under the cicada's skin, the wings are at last free to expand (*bottom*). They are crinkled like tissue paper, nothing like the rigid wings to come.

Then the cicada pulls free of its old skin. The wings unfurl and stretch fully as blood pumps into the veins. The blood then withdraws, leaving a strong structure.

At this moment in the life of a greengrocer cicada, its wings look their most brilliant — sapphire blue with emerald green veins.

The texture of the wings is similar to rippled glass. The beautiful wings remain unfurled until they dry.

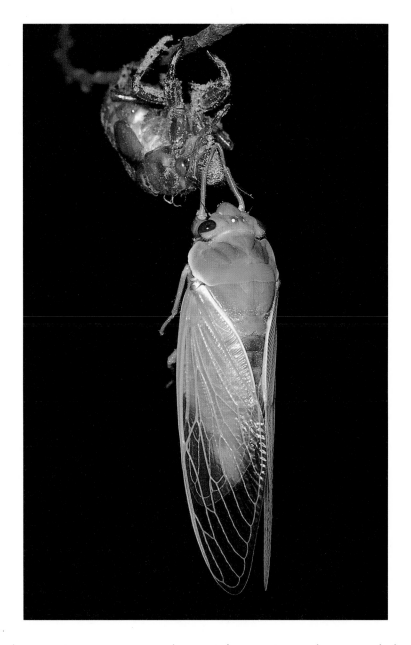

When the wings are dry, the cicada suddenly flicks them downward into their normal tent-like position (*above*). The colors start to fade. In this final stage of life, the cicada cannot afford to have bright, obvious colors that might catch the eye of a bird.

For the same reason, the red-eye cicada (*above*) does not have eye-catching colors. Its ruby-red eyes are the only outstanding, colorful feature about it.

But when the red-eye first became an adult, it was blue and gold.

Daily life

Most cicadas emerge at night. The darkness protects them from predators until they are ready to fly off. A cicada takes a risk if it emerges in daylight.

The rough bark of a banksia tree will give this emerging cicada (*top and bottom*) a good foothold and hiding place until its colorful body darkens to the camouflage colors of black and brown.

A day or so after leaving its dark underground burrow, a cicada is at ease feeding on the sunlit trunk of a gum tree or trying out its new wings. If the cicada is a male, it will also try out its new song.

The activities keeping the cicada busy at this time of life include stocking up on food and finding a **mate**. It mates with another member of its **species** to start a new generation.

Each type of cicada has a certain signature song. Males of each type recognize their own song and gather together in a group. Females follow the song to find males of their own type with which to mate.

The male tones down his song when a female approaches. If she likes him, the pair will mate, often two or three times over a period of days. In between times, the female lays eggs. After mating, the male feeds and soon dies.

When cicadas die, their remains are sometimes used for food by ants (*above*).

These shells indicate it was a good season for the cicada. Most adults live only a few weeks. Toward the end of summer, the fascinating song of the cicada fades. But the chorus will soon begin again.

Glossary

antennae: a pair of thin, movable organs on the head of insects and other animals that are used for touching and smelling.

burrow (v): to dig under the ground. (n): a hole dug in the ground by a small animal for its home.

camouflage: a way of disguising something or someone to make it look like its surroundings.

eardrum: the part of the ear that vibrates when sound waves strike it.

incubator: an object that keeps a living being warm and safe.

mate (n): the male or female of a pair of animals. (v): to join together to produce young.

molt: to shed an outer covering, such as feathers, hair, or skin.

nymph: a young insect that has not yet developed into an adult.

operculi: protective covering flaps.

predator: an animal that hunts other animals for food.

resonating: producing sound vibration that is intensified and enriched.

rostrum: the beak, snout, or proboscis of various insects.

species: a group of beings with similar characteristics that are capable of mating.

tymbal: the vibrating membrane with which the male cicada produces sound.

tympani: the eardrums located on the abdomen of the cicada.

Books to Read

Animal Survival (series). Michel Barré (Gareth Stevens)

Exploring the Science of Nature (series). Jane Burton and Kim Taylor (Gareth Stevens)

Insect Metamorphosis: From Egg to Adult. Ron and Nancy Goor (Macmillan)

Insects. Laurence Mound (Eyewitness)

Insects. Steve Parker (Eyewitness)

The New Creepy Crawly Collection (series). (Gareth Stevens)

Young Naturalist Field Guides (series). (Gareth Stevens)

Videos

Critter Songs: A Celebration of Children and Wildlife. (The Video Project)

Language Without Words. (Phoenix/BFA)

The Magic Place: Animals of the Wild. (GPN)

The Untamed Wild. (Acorn Media)

Wild Animals Adapt. (AIMS)

Web Sites

www.ento.vt.edu/Facilities/OnCampus/IDLab/cicada/fs-17cic.html

www.adventure.com/encyclopedia/bug/rficicad.html

www.sover.net/%7Evtwdmag/knots.html

Index

abdomens 2, 13
antennae 2, 10

burrows 16, 17, 18, 27

camouflage 7, 26
cherry nose 10
coloring 6, 7, 22, 23, 24, 25, 26

drinking tubes 8, 9

eardrums 4, 12
ears 4, 12
egg-placers 14
eggs 2, 13, 14, 15, 16, 28
eyes 2, 11, 24

females 12, 13, 14, 27, 28

greengrocers 6, 9, 15, 22

legs 2, 10, 18, 19, 20

males 3, 12, 13, 27, 28
mating 27, 28
molting 16, 19
muscles 10

nymphs 2, 16, 17

ocelli 2, 11
operculi 2, 12, 13
ovipositors 14

predators 16, 26

red-eyes 8, 24, 25
rostrums 2, 9, 10, 16, 20

sap 8, 10
skin (shell) 3, 18, 19, 20, 21, 29
smell, sense of 10
songs 3, 4, 5, 6, 7, 13, 27, 28, 29

tymbals 2, 12, 13
tympani 2, 12, 13

wings 2, 14, 19, 20, 21, 22, 23, 27

For a free color catalog describing Gareth Stevens Publishing's list of high-quality books and multimedia programs, call 1-800-542-2595 (USA) or 1-800-461-9120 (Canada). Gareth Stevens Publishing's Fax: (414) 225-0377. See our catalog, too, on the World Wide Web: http://gsinc.com

The publisher would like to extend special thanks to Jan W. Rafert, Curator of Primates and Small Mammals, Milwaukee County Zoo, Milwaukee, Wisconsin, for his kind and professional help with the information in this book.

Library of Congress Cataloging-in-Publication Data

Clyne, Densey.
 Cicada sing-song / by Densey Clyne.
  p. cm. — (Nature close-ups)
 "First published in 1992 by Allen & Unwin Pty Ltd . . . Australia" — T.p. verso.
 Includes bibliographical references and index.
 Summary: Introduces the physical characteristics, life cycle, and behavior of this noisy little insect.
  ISBN 0-8368-2057-6 (lib. bdg.)
  1. Cicadas—Juvenile literature.
 [1. Cicadas.] I. Title. II. Series: Clyne, Densey. Nature close-ups.
 QL527.C5C59 1998
 595.752—dc21   97-35497

First published in North America in 1998 by
Gareth Stevens Publishing
1555 North RiverCenter Drive
Suite 201
Milwaukee, WI 53212 USA

First published in 1992 by Allen & Unwin Pty Ltd, 9 Atchison Street, St. Leonards, NSW 2065, Australia.

Text and photographs © 1992 by Densey Clyne. Additional end matter © 1998 by Gareth Stevens, Inc.

Printed in the United States of America

1 2 3 4 5 6 7 8 9 02 01 00 99 98